1970s CHILDHOOD

Liza Hollinghurst

SHIRE PUBLICATIONS

Bloomsbury Publishing Plc
PO Box 883, Oxford, OX1 9PL, UK
1385 Broadway, 5th Floor, New York, NY 10018, USA

E-mail: shire@bloomsbury.com

www.shirebooks.co.uk

SHIRE is a trademark of Osprey Publishing Ltd

First published in Great Britain in 2019

A catalogue record for this book is available from the British Library.

ISBN: PB 978 1 78442 328 5

     eBook 978 1 78442 329 2

     ePDF 978 1 78442 330 8

     XML 978 1 78442 331 5

19 20 21 22 23   10 9 8 7 6 5 4 3 2 1

Typeset by PDQ Digital Media Solutions, Bungay, UK.

Printed and bound in India by Replika Press Private Ltd.

Shire Publications supports the Woodland Trust, the UK's leading woodland conservation charity.

COVER IMAGE
Front cover: Familiar toys from the 1970s: a spinning top and a space hopper. (iStock)

TITLE PAGE IMAGE
A happy trio wearing typical children's fashions of the day: 'T'-bar sandals and socks, shorts and casual tops, and a floral mini dress. (Jan Gardner)

CONTENTS PAGE IMAGE
A blast from the past: Spangles packaging! (Image courtesy of www.ayrshirehistory.com)

ACKNOWLEDGEMENTS
Thank you to the following for allowing me to share your memories: Gilly Ballard, Rachel Coburn, Mark Hollinghurst, Jill Lewis, Yvette Ryland, Rebecca Scutt, Emma Williams, and – last but not least – my parents Alan and Victoria Kitchener. Thanks also to Anne Banerji and Jan Gardner for allowing their personal family photographs to be reproduced in this book. Particular thanks go to my commissioning editor Russell Butcher for giving me the opportunity to write this book and for patiently putting up with my seemingly endless synopses. Finally, a very special thank you to Kit Williams for generously sharing memories of his book *Masquerade*.

DEDICATION
For Jessamy. This is your mum's childhood.

SUPER FRUIT FLAVOURS

SPANGLES

CONTENTS

INTRODUCTION 4

WELCOME HOME: FAMILY LIFE 7

THE BEST DAYS OF YOUR LIFE: SCHOOL 13

EXTRA HELPINGS: FOOD AND DRINK 21

RUNNING FREE: RECREATION 27

PAGE-TURNERS: BOOKS AND MAGAZINES 34

SWITCHED ON: TELEVISION 41

THE BEAT GOES ON: POPULAR MUSIC 49

YOU WEAR IT WELL: FASHION 55

EPILOGUE 61

FURTHER READING 61

IMAGE ACKNOWLEDGEMENTS 62

PLACES TO VISIT 63

INDEX 64

INTRODUCTION

Eavesdrop into any conversation about a 1970s childhood and the reminiscences will pop up: the 'Can you remember…?' and 'Did you have a…?' For those whose formative years span the decade it invariably evokes nostalgic memories of when a pocket full of Spangles would sustain a road trip cycling around recreation fields; of acrylic tank tops, the Wombles wombling free and those school holidays that seemed blessed with endless hot summers. For some, such memories will ring true with those good times out-weighing the bad that have gradually ebbed away over the years, leaving a rose-tinted retrospective view. However, others will recall the 1970s as a time of both economic and familial deprivation, and of being amongst the 'have nots' instead of the 'haves'.

The idealised family unit of 2.4 children, well-dressed and cosily living in a semi-detached house with all mod-cons on a brand-new estate and a smart Morris Marina on the drive, as often depicted in magazine and television adverts, was far out of reach for many. The reality was that the jobs weren't available – even for willing and skilled workers. Towns and cities founded on industry floundered in the recession; equally, those who were lucky enough to be employed had to stretch the family finances, which meant that certain memorable toys, foodstuffs and fashions that comprise numerous childhood reminiscences for some, are missing for others. These might be the children whose parents had to make the difficult decision of whether to go on strike with fellow union members or continue working to keep a roof over their family's head and run the barrage of abuse and shouts of 'Scab' when they arrived for work each morning or shift. The childish excitement from having to use candles during the power cuts was a novelty as there was the parental surety that the lights (and telly) would eventually go back on again. For some children, however, this lack of power was a commonplace situation if there weren't enough coins to go into the electricity meter; there was nothing exciting about that.

Each chapter of this book concentrates on a common thread throughout childhood: the food eaten, the music listened to and the games played. It would have been easy to focus upon the good times and present an entertaining, idealised lifestyle, but a more balanced view of the decade is offered here, written with the author's first-hand experiences and observations from fellow '70s children, thus presenting an insight of what daily life was like for the average child.

TIMELINE

1970: The chewy chocolate delight that is Curly Wurly goes on sale.

1971: First *Two Ronnies* episode is aired in April and sets a precedent for Saturday night family viewing for years to come.

1972: Mark II Raleigh Chopper with its five-speed T-bar gear shift is a 'must have' for every speedy youngster.

1973: Released in March, Pink Floyd's *Dark Side of the Moon* album becomes a permanent fixture on elder siblings' turntables.

1974: Mayhem on television as *Tiswas* launches in January; its madcap humour appeals to children and adults alike.

1975: Roald Dahl publishes *Danny, Champion of the World*.

1976: Dance troupe Legs & Co. make their first appearance on *Top of the Pops*.

1977: Audiences feel the Force as George Lucas's *Star Wars* is screened in cinemas nationwide.

1978: Bearded Father Abraham and his blue Belgian friends arrive in the UK music charts with their *Smurf Song*.

1979: Daredevil stunt motorcyclist Eddie Kidd jumps a jaw-dropping 80 feet over a viaduct at Maldon in Essex in December.

WELCOME HOME: FAMILY LIFE

Saturday evenings meant mum doing her hair in a cloud of hairspray in the front room mirror whilst watching the Tom Jones show, then going down to the pub to watch dad play in the darts team.

Mark Hollinghurst

Two national events loom large in the memories of many children of the 1970s: the 1976 heatwave, followed by Queen Elizabeth II's Silver Jubilee in 1977. June 1976 started off nicely, the warm weather ushering what people hoped would be a long, hot summer – and what an unforgettable scorcher it would turn out to be. From June through to August, the sun relentlessly beat down upon Britain, bestowing blessings both for sun worshippers and school kids on their summer holidays, yet a curse for water authorities and gardeners. For fifteen consecutive days temperatures soared to a very un-British 32°C, baking both skin and prized garden planting; the southwest of Britain was bereft of rain for some staggering 45 days during July and August. The intense and incessant heat transformed riverbeds into a parched network of cracks worthy of a science-fiction film set and even road surfacing began to melt; prodding the gooey tarmac with a stick proved to be irresistible. Below-average rainfall for the previous twelve months exacerbated the situation. Water companies, struggling to keep up with the steep and unremitting increase

A mother and her children stand in the doorway of their home in an East London block of flats.

in demand as their reservoir levels simultaneously decreased to unprecedented lows, had no other option than to introduce water rationing in the form of standpipes in residential streets. In doing so, they inadvertently created a new and unenviable childhood task: queuing for water.

The 25th year of accession to the throne by Queen Elizabeth II was patriotically celebrated with both formal and informal events throughout 1977 in Britain and the Commonwealth. Schools also joined in and gave out commemorative mugs, coins and even bracelets to their pupils, some of whom were less than eager to receive them:

> I was given a steel identity bracelet with the Silver Jubilee logo of a crown surrounded with a laurel wreath engraved on it. I didn't wear it as I was starting to get into punk at the time and would have been mortified to have been caught wearing it.

A young local girl slips her hand between the wide cracks in the dried-up Pitsford Reservoir, Northamptonshire, in July 1976 during the peak of the heatwave.

Most celebrations were reserved for 7 June, the official date of the Silver Jubilee. The day was marked all over Britain with community events, such as street parties, fêtes, fancy dress competitions, bonfires and firework displays. Streets were decked with Union Jacks, bunting and rows of tables of chairs for communal children's picnics where families contributed food and drink; the festivities continuing well into the early hours of the following morning.

On the home front, it was evident that interior design hadn't reached the confines of many childhood bedrooms. Walls were decorated with posters and mass-produced pictures featuring large-eyed, solemn-faced children or

enlivened by gender-specific wallpaper; football or racing cars for boys, and for the girls, florals or poke-bonneted Holly Hobbie. Furniture was likely to be second-hand, with single beds made up with candy-striped brushed cotton sheets, blankets from Brentford Nylons, all topped off

'God Save the Queen' – Salford residents celebrate the Silver Jubilee of Queen Elizabeth II with a huge street party.

with a candlewick bedspread and a much-loved Chad Valley teddy. 'My friend had a duvet with Snoopy on it. I was envious and thought it was the height of sophistication. It made my bed look frumpy in comparison.' The numerous power cuts that blighted the decade and frustrated parents were an adventure for children, providing a new lighting source to many bedrooms: a candle in a jam jar. This added a frisson of excitement at bedtimes as books were read by candlelight and torchlight-beam battles were fought on bedroom ceilings, all set against the smell of a paraffin heater elsewhere in the house.

This was also a time where parents could leave a baby or toddler outside a shop in a pushchair and have no concerns about their safety or being reported to Social Services. Multiple prams neatly lined up in front of a shop was a common sight in Britain's high streets, although some forgetful or otherwise occupied mums walked off without collecting their offspring:

I left the baby outside Woolworths and for some reason completely forgot about her when I walked out. I was half-way down the street when I remembered and hurried back to find her happily cooed over by two old ladies.

Mirror, mirror... A teenager's bedroom typical of the decade with its posters, shelves of furry toys and hand-me-down furniture.

Though advertising depicted the stereotypical family as happy and comfortably well off by the day's standards, the 1970s saw the traditional family unit of 2.4 children being chipped away, aided by legislation in the form of the 1969 Divorce Reform Act, which came into effect in 1971. This Act was crucial in providing women with the chance to free themselves from failing or abusive relationships that they would otherwise have stayed in. Individuals could now divorce their spouses without having to prove which party was at 'fault', i.e. due to adultery or desertion, on condition that the marriage proved to have irretrievably broken down. Though divorce had its benefits, life as a single parent was a struggle and the financial impact significant, which led to an increase in child poverty as parents tried to keep their families afloat whilst living on the breadline. Women who worked had to contend with the fact that they received 35 percent less in their weekly wage packets than men, an aspect that the Finer Report on One-Parent Families (1974) identified in conjunction with other socio-economic factors affecting single-parent families. The Finer Report highlighted the plight of these families and associated child poverty, its findings contributing towards the 1975 Child Benefit Act. Families also experienced a role reversal, as the recession and increasing rates of unemployment resulted in some fathers temporarily staying at home to look after the children while their wives found temporary employment to tide the family over, as one stay-at-home dad remembers:

I was made redundant from my engineering job in 1973 and had to look after my toddler while her mother found work as a factory seamstress. Luckily, I became employed six months later. Many of my friends were in the same situation as me so it wasn't unusual at the time.

The continuing political violence known as the Troubles and the conflict between nationalists and unionists compounded by events of Bloody Sunday (30 January 1972) seriously affected children in Northern Ireland. Burnt-out cars, set amongst buildings painted with murals depicting political and religious affiliations, became rusty playthings. Segregated residential roads were 'no go' areas if your family was of a different political or religious persuasion to those who lived there, while car bombs and stray fire from military and terrorist sections were deadly to children passing by or the curious poking their heads around a wall. Home wasn't a safe place either, as terrorist retribution for family members thought to be informers or 'grasses' was unforgiving, brutal and fatal. This and the search for a safer place to live caused many families to set new roots over the Irish Sea in counties like Lancashire: 'One morning at primary school a new kid turned up in class. He was from Northern Ireland and his house had been bombed.' Religious division even spread to the mainland, as one former schoolboy remembers:

This was a time when a mum felt she could safely leave her baby in its pushchair outside a shop while she did her shopping.

Catholics and Protestants from separate schools would clash on the street. These could be small scuffles or bigger fights with between thirty and fifty kids shouting and scrapping. It got to be such a problem that the individual schools staggered start and end times to avoid these situations.

THE BEST DAYS OF YOUR LIFE: SCHOOL

In sewing lessons, us girls learnt embroidery using a fabric called *Binca*, stitching in cross-stitch with huge plastic needles and an array of coloured threads.

Rebecca Scutt

Although this was the decade of experimental 'free' schools run by non-conformists who radically did away with the national curriculum and celebrated individuality, attendance at the local primary followed by secondary school was the norm for the majority of youngsters and an inevitability for nearly every child. No matter how limpet-hard you clung onto your mum on the first day of primary school or how long you spent in the classroom hiccupping back the tears, the reality was that your parents had just clocked you into a fourteen-year educational stretch that no amount of good behaviour could exempt you from. These first-day experiences have become indelibly etched into many memories: 'I remember crying as mum left and then being seated next to a boy who proceeded to share his pencils in an effort to comfort me. My tears dropped onto the paper and in trying to rub them away, I scratched a big hole in my drawing. I was not happy.' Yet for others it was an exciting new experience: 'My first day at school was brilliant. I made a best friend straightaway and we bonded over Lego and football.'

Children swarming over a metal climbing frame in a school playground. Note the unsuitable footwear with plastic soles, which rendered any grip on the frame impossible.

Two girls at Edith Neville School, North London, in 1974, tucking into their fish fingers, baked beans and potato, which was apparently followed by sponge and custard for pudding.

The playground was where friendships were made, lost and regained, battles fought, innocent kisses snatched after a game of 'kiss-chase' and 'tags' slapped on the backs of those not quick enough to escape from their pursuers. Boys re-enacted war and action films, shouting out 'Ack-ack-ack' as imaginary machine guns were fired, whilst girls played games of 'elastic' with a length of sewing elastic tied with a knot and woven around the players' feet whilst they jumped and sang songs like 'Inside Out' with its refrain 'England, Ireland, Scotland, Wales – inside, outside, monkeys' tails'. It was also the place where limbs were scraped raw on bare tarmac, bones were broken from falling off climbing frames and skin was burnt to a livid shade of red that would cry out for a layer of calamine lotion at bedtime. Whereas today's playgrounds have bark or rubber soft-play areas to soften the impact from falls and all play equipment is safety checked, risk assessed and secured into the ground, those in the 1970s were accidents ready to happen.

We had a metal geodesic climbing frame at our primary school that wasn't fastened down, so you could get all the kids to climb up one side and rock it to try and lift the other side off the ground. One day a girl fell off and broke her two front teeth on the tarmac below. It wouldn't have been too bad, but they were her permanent teeth.

School dinners: love them or hate them, every former '70s child has their own opinion. While some kids went home for their lunch or took a packed lunch in a Tupperware box, others had to resort to school dinners. These could be a hit-and-miss affair and by mid-morning playtime the smells wafting from the school kitchen could determine what was going to land on the plate at lunchtime. There was the overpowering pong of boiled cabbage that would be teamed with lumpy tasteless mashed potato or – to everyone's joy – the delicious aroma of chips that would be plated up with the keenly awaited baked beans and sausages. Puddings were often traditional stodgy affairs like jam roly-poly and spotted dick, but chocolate crunch/concrete/tarmac (the name was school-dependent) has gone down in schoolkid history as the decade's legendary school pudding. This solid square slab of brown cake with its crispy sugared top adorned with pink custard is what many fond school memories were made of. [Author's Note: I have it on good authority that the custard was made using strawberry blancmange

The slogan 'Mind That Child' was emblazoned on the rear of ice cream vans in an attempt to warn motorists of the likelihood of children besieging the van as soon as its tinkling chimes could be heard in the neighbourhood.

powder.] Tuck shops were also a vital part of school life, selling penny sweets like Black Jacks and Fruit Salads, those all-important crisps and soft drinks that came in plastic cups with a straw with which to pierce the lid. Canny ice cream van operators also targeted this eager juvenile market, rolling up outside the school gates at lunchtime for their clientele to order a Cider Quench or Screwball.

The academic face of schools has considerably changed since the 1970s, particularly the classrooms. Whereas technology in the form of interactive whiteboards and mobile electronic devices such as tablets are now commonplace, the '70s schoolchild was educated using teaching aids that hadn't evolved much in form. The traditional wooden desks with their retired inkwells and hinged desktops were still commonplace in primary and secondary schools; but now adorned with years of biro-ingrained graffiti, from the names of pop groups and football teams through to the ubiquitous 'Karen loves Dave 4 Ever', which inevitably ended up being scribbled out months later. The blackboard had been somewhat updated and was now found on a roller similar to a blind, which the teacher

The class joker being told to sit back down by an unimpressed teacher. In the background is a roller blackboard, a common sight in classrooms.

could pull down in the morning to find a cheeky epithet chalked on it by an unknown joker – much to the hilarity of the assembled class and anger of the aforementioned teacher. The wooden board-rubber with its felt base unwittingly

A penny for them. The tedium of school is evident in the face of this daydreaming youngster.

provided the annoyed teacher with a useful corrective weapon to add to their existing corporal punishment arsenal of cane and plimsoll (as attested by the miscreants who found themselves on the receiving end of an airborne board-rubber launched at their head). Yet one of the longstanding tenets of education, mental arithmetic, was facing a particular challenge from the onset of the decade's electronic age: the pocket calculator. With its liquid crystal display (LCD) the calculator was a must-have on the Christmas lists of many children during the mid- to late 1970s. Though banned from the classroom, a calculator could still be used to work out those tricky homework questions that once would have baffled the school's less numerate pupils.

Morning assemblies were, more often than not, bum-numbingly boring affairs – unless the guilty parties caught graffitiing on the school shed or writing rude words on a teacher's dirty car had been apprehended and paraded in front of the school as punishment. Music was in the form of hymns accompanied by a teacher plonking out the notes on the out-of-tune school piano; songs were picked out of the BBC's *Come and Praise* hymnal, which featured '*Kumbaya*', '*He's Got the Whole World in His Hands*' and 'modern' hymns like '*When I Needed a Neighbour*' and '*Lord of the Dance*'.

Loved by some, hated by others: the mid-morning milk break pre-'Milk Snatcher' years.

One important school issue that divided both children and politicians was milk. It was then Conservative Education Secretary Margaret Thatcher who in 1971 controversially decided to cease free milk for primary school children aged seven and above, gaining her the infamous 'Milk Snatcher' moniker. To some children this would have been perceived as a blessing, as starting the day with milk warmed up from having been left out in the sun was unappetising:

> I forced down as much milk as I could literally swallow and then clasping my hands around the bottle to hide the remainder, tried to put it back in the crate without the teacher seeing. She soon caught onto my ruse and made sure I finished my milk each day afterwards. I haven't been able to drink milk since.

The final death knell for free school milk was rung in 1977 when the Labour government abolished milk for the under-sevens.

The school leaving age had been raised from fifteen to sixteen in 1972, closely followed by the Education (Work Experience) Act 1973, which sought to provide work experience for children under school-leaving age as part of their education and to prepare them for future employment. Yet the 1973–75 recession, compounded by the Three-Day Week and industrial action, all posed adverse challenges to school leavers trying to find their way in a job market where even the most skilled worker couldn't find continuous employment. With the estimated number of industrial action disputes rapidly peaking between 1970 and 1972, it was no wonder that pupils disheartened with how bleak their employment chances looked and frustrated with the 'old-fashioned' authoritarian stance taken by schools over uniforms and continued use of corporal punishment, decided to take a leaf out of their elders' 'work to rule' book and hold their own strikes. The touchpaper was first lit on 4 May 1972 when approximately two hundred male pupils at Quintin Kynaston School in North London walked out in protest over school dinners, caning and the conformity of school uniforms. Following in their footsteps a few days later, a group of sixty pupils started out on an 8-mile protest march; however, this was only the start, as the strikes culminated in a thousand-pupil-strong demonstration march in London against the use of corporal punishment, respectively organised by the Schools' Action Union and the National Union of School Students. Despite this collective pupil solidarity and the high-profile demos, it took a further fourteen years for corporal punishment to be banned in state-run schools.

Defiant schoolgirls in Hyde Park taking part in the demonstration against caning in schools held on 7 May 1972.

EXTRA HELPINGS: FOOD AND DRINK

Growing up in Ireland in the 1970s we didn't have much and didn't expect much; Dublin was run down and depressing. Our big treat was a packet of Tayto and a Fanta once a week.

Jill Lewis

Memories are made of food and drink: school dinners, Friday night fish and chips, homemade fizzy pop and the chocolate bar that now seems a lot smaller than when you were a child. A bag from a discontinued brand of crisps, now a museum exhibit, can bring back waves of nostalgia; similarly, retro dinner plates with their orange and brown patterns so beloved in the decade, can summon up reminiscences of a mum's celebrated Sunday roast or a convenience food 'treat' of chow mein.

Whereas their parents' childhood may have been overshadowed by wartime sweet rationing which ended in 1953, '70s children had no such restrictions. They gloried in an abundance of sugary confectionery that met with the approval of even the most discerning juvenile palates. It was a time when every town had a sweet shop choc-a-bloc full of sweets in all forms. With its serried rainbow ranks of sweet jars and its counter stacked with chocolate bars, presided over by an eagle-eyed shopkeeper who could simultaneously serve whilst monitoring a light-fingered clientele, the

Getting busy with the fizzy: SodaStream, the must-have fizzy drinks maker.

temptations of the sweet shop loomed large. A former customer recalls the dilemma of childhood budgeting:

> You could buy brown chocolate mice for ½p each and fill a whole paper bag for 5p – my entire pocket money. White chocolate mice were much tastier and bigger but cost 1p each, so it was a choice of quality or quantity.

As television found its way into more homes, adverts promoting sweets, snack foods and soft drinks were broadcast on commercial stations during breaks in children's programmes, their catchy tunes and slogans unconsciously worming their way into the memory banks of their captive young audiences. From the nursery rhyme refrain of a 'finger of fudge' through to Nestlé's bespectacled Milky Bar Kid exclaiming 'The Milky Bars are on me!', children's spending and pester power was eagerly targeted by advertising agencies. No matter how funny and appealing the ads were, however, there was a significant and painful downside. Sweets combined with the high sugar content in fruit squashes and fizzy drinks contributed to a staggeringly high percentage of dental caries in both milk and secondary teeth. In 1973, 93 percent of twelve-year-old children in England and Wales were found to have tooth decay, compared with 34 percent in England, Wales and Northern Ireland in 2013. The increase in fluoride being added to toothpaste which by 1978 comprised 96 percent of toothpastes on the UK market, in conjunction with parental education via the Health Education Council and dental care taught in school, helped to gradually lower this percentage.

An impromptu picnic for these two with their bottles of pop.

The 1970s is a decade infamous for its political incorrectness and this extended to childhood too. Candy versions of cigarettes and Spanish Gold 'Sweet Tobacco' made from coconut were widely available, with a Christmas stocking favourite being a realistic packet of paper-wrapped chocolate cigars. Parents didn't think twice about whether this could encourage their offspring to try smoking at a later date as

Sparking up. Youthful smokers who have evidently swapped candy cigarettes for the real thing.

their kids swaggered round aping their elders or just happily munched their way through a packet. Correspondingly, it was also a time when a child could go into the local newsagents and buy cigarettes ostensibly for a parent; cans of Shandy Bass could similarly be obtained from the corner shop – no questions asked.

Traditional 'meat and two veg' weekday dinners prepared from fresh food had been challenged in previous decades by the advent of pre-packed convenience food and frozen products. By the 1970s the trend for packaged 'cook-straight-from-the-box/bag' foods was still on the rise and perceived as essentials to add to the weekly or daily visit to the supermarket. The attraction of such meals was that they were quick and easy to prepare, a boon for those women who worked yet also had to get the family's dinner ready when they arrived home. Frozen fish fingers and beef burgers were now appearing on dinner plates to the enjoyment of many youngsters:

> Our fridge had the world's tiniest ice box, just big enough for the very latest in convenience food: a box of just six frozen fish fingers. This went around a family of four and I can only assume they were bigger in the Seventies.

A complete family meal could be 'cooked' in a matter of minutes using both frozen and dehydrated foodstuffs.

Dehydrated products were just as popular as their frozen counterparts when it came to convenience, bringing with them new flavours and an element of space-age excitement. Instant mashed potato courtesy of Cadbury's 'Smash' (as advertised by derisive laughing metal aliens) was plated up alongside crispy pancakes and peas accompanied by a glass of orange-flavoured water made from powdered orange juice. Pudding could be a slice of Arctic Roll or a dessert whipped up in moments from a packet of Angel Delight; creative mums jazzed theirs up with sprinkles, sponge fingers or grated chocolate.

Families began eating out more and whilst an Indian or Chinese restaurant might have been perceived as 'forbidden fruit' for some children, there were plenty of places where a family meal could be enjoyed. Fish and chips continued to be a perennial favourite, eaten in the chip shop seating area or in the car on a rainy afternoon with the steamed-up windows ready to be drawn on with greasy fingers. For a special event like a birthday, the Berni Inn was the place to go. Marketed as a steakhouse, the Berni seemed very sophisticated to a youngster, with its menu filled with tempting delicacies like prawn cocktail, steak and chips, and Black Forest gateau.

When it came to school lunchboxes and snacking between meals, the crisp aficionado had the widest assortment of brands and eclectic flavours to choose from – a curious few being Bovril, chutney, sweet 'n' sour, pickled onion and even 'bat-burger'. Two companies battling it out at the top of the potato pile were Golden Wonder with their innovative flavours and packet design, who showered young crisp consumers with ranges like

Schoolboys eating their lunch of chips in April 1971 as school meals were not being served due to a pay dispute.

Horror Bags and Rock 'n Rollers, and Smiths, who countered back with monster-feet-shaped Monster Munch and Kung Fuey crisps, the Bruce Lee inspired packet design appealing to playground martial arts fans. Coincidently, there was also a craze for shrinking crisps bags in a hot oven to miniaturise them; known as 'shrinkies', these were used to make jewellery, keyrings and bookmarks.

When it came to childhood beverages, the decade was owned by cans and bottles of fizzy pop, often in lurid colours and with a high sugar content. It was decidedly cool to cycle down the street on a Raleigh Chopper, flares flapping in the breeze whilst nonchalantly swigging from a cola bottle. Popular brands included Corona, Panda Pops and Cresta, whose advertising campaign comprised a cartoon polar bear wearing sunglasses with the catchphrase, 'It's frothy, man!' Usually children aren't interested in kitchen gadgets, but when it came to the must-have SodaStream parents were cajoled to buy one and 'Get busy with the fizzy'. Just two pushes of a button magically turned a bottle of water into fizz with the aid of carbon dioxide gas and a splash of coloured artificial flavouring. Milk producers fought back against this fizzy drink onslaught, aided by magazine and television adverts that extolled the health benefits of the daily pinta.

The freedom of two wheels. This young miss looks very content with her Raleigh bike with its bell and pannier ready to carry home sweets and comics from a trip to the newsagent.

Unigate's ad campaign was one of the most memorable, featuring comedians Sid James, Arthur Mullard and Spike Milligan – even the decade's eminent athlete, Muhammed Ali – all warning milk-drinkers to 'Watch out, there's a Humphrey about' ready to steal their milk. The 'Humphrey' character was Unigate's invisible milk drinker of unknown appearance except for its red and white stripy straw, which it sneakily dipped into the glasses of milk held by the celebrity endorsers in the adverts.

RUNNING FREE: RECREATION

One of my favourite Christmas presents was 'Chip Away'. The premise was that you had a lump of 'stone' that you chipped away at with a mini mallet and a chisel to reveal a 'sculpture'. The stone was some kind of waxy material and when you chipped it, it went all over the place. It was a proper mess and quite tedious, but worth the reward of the rearing horse figurine.

Emma Williams

The run-up to Christmas started with nose-to-glass perusal of heavily stocked toy shop window displays, scanning the television adverts and flicking through the Woolworths and Green Shield Stamps catalogues, set against a soundtrack of Slade's '*Merry Xmas Everybody*' (1973) and Greg Lake's '*I Believe in Father Christmas*' (1975). Many youngsters, the author included, were only setting themselves up for a fall after writing a lengthy list for Santa and finding few of their desired toys wrapped up under the tree thanks to the 1973–75 recession, which saw unemployment figures rise, numerous industrial disputes and high inflation. Many parents had to resort to a 'make do and mend' ethos to supplement their children's presents: 'My dad made me a ride-on steam train out of a catering-sized coffee tin, a wooden box and pram wheels, which I loved freewheeling downhill into the cul-de-sac without any kind of brakes.'

Children playing on a home-made go-cart outside a corner shop in Manchester, 1977. Above them is a traffic sign designating a play street.

Making a mental note for his Christmas list is this lad checking out the model railway on display at Hamley's toy shop in London.

Children had a vast range of toys available to them, especially due to the significant increase in those mass-produced and imported from China or Taiwan; many of them had the exciting attribute of innovative electronic components that made them bleep and flash, such as Simon, produced by American company Milton Bradley, which comprised a memory game whereby the players had to duplicate a pattern of electronically generated lights and sounds. Traditional British-made wooden toys that had faithfully served generations were now losing out to their foreign counterparts in a toy market that was becoming saturated with cheap and visually engaging imports. Companies such as Palitoy and Pedigree, who had out-sourced their manufacturing overseas, produced a significant proportion of the toys sold in Britain and their thriving profits enabled their budgets to absorb product development, marketing and licensing costs; Palitoy secured the licensing rights to produce toys under the Star Wars brand, a move that would prove to be enormously profitable. The decade would see both companies producing toys, especially dolls – or 'action figures', as the male version became known – that would not only cement their position in British marketing but also in the memories of many youngsters.

Based on the GI Joe action figure manufactured by American brand Hasbro, Palitoy launched its own British version, Action Man, in 1966 under licence from Hasbro. By the mid-1970s, Action Man was deployed into numerous toy cupboards nationwide, ready to take on any adventure – from being launched out of a bedroom window, surviving concrete-scarred playground battles or reluctantly getting 'married' to Palitoy's other popular doll Pippa or Pedigree love rival, Sindy (Britain's answer to her American cousin, Barbie). In comparison to the glamorous and adventurous Barbie with

OPPOSITE:
An array of toys including Action Man, Scalextric, Girl's World, Sindy, Connect Four and Simon.

Boys playing at the inner-city Notting Hill Adventure Playground in London, 1972. Local open access adventure playgrounds like this were promoted in an attempt to reduce crime and to reach disillusioned youngsters.

her California-cool wardrobe, Blighty's Sindy was more 'girl-next-door' with her equestrian and ballet outfits. Television tie-ins also contributed to the toy market, with Action Man challenged by the Six Million Dollar Man with his magnifying eye and roll-back 'skin' that hid the 'bionics' in his arm; cue schoolboys using felt-tip pens to draw bionics onto their own arms. Girls also had their own version, the Bionic Woman, with her long blonde hair and blue jumpsuit – the perfect companion to their 'boyfriend's' action figure.

Other toys worthy of mention are the much-loved Lego and Scalextric, Girl's World styling head (which often ended up with hacked-off hair) and the rotund orange rubber Spacehopper that spent its last years deflated in the garden shed. For the daring, there were 'clackers' – two plastic balls connected by a length of string. These were wielded with great dexterity by playground show-offs, akin to Bruce Lee with his nunchucks – at the risk of either cracking themselves on the knuckles or some unfortunate bystander in the head. 'When they came out I can remember seeing lots of kids with bandaged and bruised wrists', remembers one playground observer.

Collections were popular in the 1970s. Stamp collecting remained a widespread hobby amongst both boys and girls, but bedrooms were starting to become inhabited by colourful and intriguing *objets d'art*. Nude plastic gonks with their shock of luridly coloured 'hair' stared down from shelves, and neat rows of tiny pottery animal figurines branded as Whimsies by manufacturer Wade were lined up on bookcases or windowsills. Other collections included beer mats, football stickers, bubble-gum and cigarette cards, Matchbox cars, Hot Rod racers, Airfix models, and free gifts given away with breakfast cereals and other foodstuffs.

What most 1970s children fondly recollect is the freedom of playing outside away from home and parental supervision, cycling off to explore the neighbourhood's legitimate and illicit delights. This wasn't even perceived as freedom then. It was just something that children did without thinking of any consequences and parents were perfectly happy with it, as long as they

knew roughly where their children were and if they'd be back home in time for lunch or dinner. City youngsters had an urban playground of derelict houses, wasteland that hadn't been developed since the Second World War, canals, municipal parks – even railway lines. Their rural peers similarly had free run of fields, woods, rivers and derelict cottages. 'I remember camping in the mountains, building dens and dams, and wild swimming in the River Taff', recalls one nature child of her Welsh childhood. Territorial dens, built from whatever materials lay to hand or recycled from derelict buildings, were regularly subject to being wrecked by raiding parties from other gangs who, in turn, had their own dens ruined in honourable retaliation.

'Your go!' Intense concentration on the faces of these two players of popular Milton Bradley game, Downfall.

Bikes at the ready and nonchalantly blowing a bubblegum bubble, this girl looks set for a cycle trip in the sunshine.

The heatwave of 1976, which dramatically saw temperatures rise and reservoir levels fall, was childhood bliss and enticed youngsters into swimming and paddling in streams, rivers and canals to cool off. Yet this freedom came with its own set of dangers, which were acknowledged by the government and publicised via public information films by the Central Office of Information. These films were broadcast during children's television programming and the fact that their content can still be recalled decades later reflects how hard-hitting and often scary they were.

The dangerous yet exciting urban playground of derelict houses left over from slum clearances and bomb damage from the Second World War.

In *Lonely Water* (1973) a menacing hooded figure is seen waiting alongside a misty lake with Donald Pleasance's narration eerily intoning, 'I am the Spirit of Dark and Lonely Water, ready to trap the unwary, the show-off, the fool, and this is the kind of place you'd expect to find me.' Another film highlighting the hazards of fatal house fires from children playing with matches follows an unseen person making their way through a fire-damaged house, whilst echoing children's voices call out in distress. Others warned of becoming blinded by fireworks, flying kites near electricity pylons, playing in old fridges, even retrieving a frisbee from an electricity substation. Animations were also used to promote safety, notably those featuring a little boy called Tony who is stopped from going off with strangers, playing with matches or going near boiling saucepans by his garrulous ginger cat Charley. Celebrity footballer Kevin Keegan and the future Darth Vader, Dave 'Green Cross Code Man' Prowse, featured in campaigns teaching road safety to child pedestrians.

A young boy tending his campfire in Norfolk, 1976.

The cinema was as popular as ever for family recreation and the decade would famously play host to the cinematic highpoint of George Lucas's science fiction adventure *Star Wars* (1977), which broke box-office records worldwide and still remains one of highest earning films to date. Premiered in London on 27 December, *Star Wars* rapidly became the must-see film, its popularity accelerated by merchandise, comics and playground gossip. The excitement it generated amongst children was palpable:

Star Wars – the film that launched hundreds of thousands of plastic figures of Princess Leia, Han Solo, Luke Skywalker and Chewbacca, amongst other characters.

> My mum took me to see *Star Wars* and I remember that when the caption started everyone in the cinema began to read it out together. Then the words went off into space and we were waiting. There was a planet, a small ship then that huge spaceship moved across the screen as if it were flying over us. The sound of it shook the cinema and the whole place erupted. We were shouting, cheering and standing up in the seats and that's pretty much how it went on throughout the film.

After a month's showing in London almost 600,000 people had seen the film – a phenomenal attendance rate. *Star Wars* had such an impact on many youthful imaginations that even today there are those who are still rapt by the franchise and have over the decades added to their *Star Wars* collections of toys, memorabilia and other collectables.

PAGE-TURNERS: BOOKS AND MAGAZINES

> My favourite books were the Ladybird series, especially fairy tales such as *The Princess and the Pea* with the scary page showing the very dishevelled princess standing at the doorway in a raging thunderstorm repeatedly claiming to be a real princess.
>
> Rebecca Scutt

Children's literature flourished during the decade thanks to an increased awareness of the importance of literacy within the educational curriculum brought about by the 1975 Bullock Report *A Language for Life*, in conjunction with the abundant publishing of books aimed at all reading ages. Although timeless authors like Enid Blyton, Richmal Crompton and E. Nesbit still retained their place on the bookshelf, the mid-1970s saw a prolific rise in new fiction. In 1976, the book publishing industry had grown by 25 percent in just five years; this was aided by high-quality and imaginative contemporary children's fiction and also an upsurge in paperback publishing due to financial restrictions affecting Local Authority libraries in 1976. Dwindling funds from public coffers caused library budgets to be significantly slashed, which in turn meant that previously favoured and more expensive hardback books were now discarded for cheaper paperbacks, whereby two or more copies of a book could be bought for the cost of a single hardback.

Young habitués of the local library or bookshop now had a greater and contemporary choice of storybooks to read, many of which are now acknowledged as classic children's fiction. Roald Dahl reigned supreme: whilst ensconced in his Great Missenden writing hut he fashioned and composed his beloved books for 'chiddlers' with enduring characters, such as *Charlie and the Great Glass Elevator* (1974). Other notable well-thumbed classics included *Watership Down* (1972) by Richard Adams, *The Diddakoi* (1972) by Rumer Godden, and Nina Bawden's *Carrie's War* (1973).

That perpetual children's favourite, the hardback Ladybird book, continued to hold a relevant place in the 1970s education system with its alpha-numeric 'Key Words Reading Scheme', which introduced the reader to sibling characters Peter and Jane, and pet dog Pat. The scheme's premise was simple: one page would feature the text in an easy-to-read sans serif font whilst the facing page would comprise an accompanying colourful illustration that reflected the

E. Nesbit's *The Railway Children* was just one of the classic children's books adapted into film. In the 1970 version, Gary Warren played Peter, his perky sister Bobbie was played by Jenny Agutter, and Phyllis by Sally Thomsett.

Young bookworms rifle through picture books in a London library in 1976.

activity or people described. As well as the Key Words series, Ladybird books also included much-loved fairy stories in the form of *Cinderella*, *Sleeping Beauty* and *Rumpelstiltskin* and non-fiction subjects like history, science, social studies and hobbies. The books' intrinsic qualities in the form of bold fonts and eye-catching illustrations appealed to children and parents alike, their relatively few pages less off-putting than a weightier tome.

Early-reading and picture books aimed at pre-school and reception age children which captured infant attention were essential for publishers, especially when considering the market appeal for parents looking for books to give their children a head start. Entertaining illustrations, be they simple or detailed, were the key to visual and intellectual engagement with both parents and children, and many books have remained childhood favourites, enduring the literary test of

time, to be fondly re-read to future generations. One prime example is the 'Mr Men' series, written and illustrated by Roger Hargreaves, which made a first appearance with the wriggly-armed *Mr Tickle* in 1971; in all, forty-nine books were published in the series. The ageless simplicity of Hargreaves' books, their loveable characters and small, tactile soft-back size perfect for little hands, easily merited him a devoted following of readers, and later, lucrative licensing for a variety of merchandise. Yet, the most important and lasting legacy that Hargreaves bequeathed after his early death in 1988 was imparting a love of books and reading into generations of children.

Roger Hargreaves gets in step with two of his creations, Mr Happy and Little Miss Scatterbrain.

The comic remained a staple weekly purchase throughout the decade, with treasured stalwarts *The Beano* and *The Dandy* still as popular as ever with boys and girls. Gender-neutral *Look-in* appeared on newsagents' shelves in 1971 and with its ITV-based content was mooted as the junior equivalent of *TV Times* – though obviously trendier than its sedate older sibling. *Look-in*'s content included the latest popular television series such as *On The Buses* and *The Six Million Dollar Man*, programme listings, competitions, pop star pin-ups and features on sports personalities like James Hunt and Kevin Keegan.

Comics and magazines primarily aimed at boys leant heavily on either sports (*Shoot! Goal* and *Roy of the Rovers*) or warfare (*Warlord* and *Valiant*); all perceived as 'appropriate' masculine reading for both pre-teen and teenage boys. US-based Marvel Comics with their graphic novels featuring science-fiction and superhero-based storylines and dynamic illustrations gave these traditional comics a run for their money and led to the advent of Marvel UK in 1972.

Girls had a wide choice when it came to comics. For pre-teen readers there were *Twinkle*, *Mandy* and *Bunty* with their innocuous stories of dolls' hospitals, school life and ballet: '*Bunty* often had cut-out dolls with paper clothes that you could dress in the latest fashions by folding little flaps over the dolls' shoulders.' For those who preferred something with more bite there was the spooky *Misty* with its cover regularly featuring a moonlit raven-haired beauty. *Misty*'s selling point was its supernatural storylines about ghosts, witches and vampires which made it seem deliciously illicit when read by torchlight under the bedcovers. However, when it came to teenage magazines the leader of the pack was, without a doubt, *Jackie*. A weekly publication since 1964, *Jackie* truly came into her own in the 1970s. Crammed full with fashion and beauty tips, quizzes, readers' true stories ('I Let My Parents Ruin Everything'), Cathy & Claire's problems page and, of course, the essential pop and rock music gossip and features, *Jackie* helped many young girls tackle the onset of puberty, first loves and, more importantly, how to correctly pluck one's eyebrows into the prerequisite arch. From out of the poster pages gleamed the fresh-faced toothsome smiles of The Osmonds and the wickedly charismatic gaze of Thin Lizzy's Phil Lynott – all indirectly responsible for leaving many bedroom walls permanently scarred with sticky tape. *Jackie* was read at the breakfast table, on the bus, surreptitiously in lessons, under the blankets and was passed on to friends and family, much to maternal annoyance: 'My cousins gave me their old copies, but my mum confiscated them because she thought *Jackie* was "inappropriate" for a twelve-year-old. I was furious.'

Possibly the biggest UK publishing sensation of the late 1970s and one of the decade's most memorable books was *Masquerade* (1979) by artist Kit Williams. The focus of the book was a conundrum: to decipher the clues hidden within the enigmatic and intricate illustrations that would steer one to the whereabouts of a golden bejewelled hare amulet crafted by Williams himself and buried in the English countryside. *Masquerade* comprised an enchanted real-life treasure hunt via its sumptuously illustrated pages, taking children on a magical journey across landscapes peopled with curious folk, animals and symbolism. Looking back, Williams recalls:

Although not specifically a children's book, it seemed to have a deep impact upon children, so much so that most people who write to me today start their letters and e-mails with 'I was a child of ten when *Masquerade* came out' and go on to say the book had a profound effect on them and they went on to become scientists, writers, artists, architects, etc. It is a great delight to me that reading *Masquerade* and studying its pictures seems to have given many children the courage and desire to explore their own creativity and they are now wanting to share that experience with their own children and so introducing a new generation to the work. This is the real treasure of *Masquerade*!

SWITCHED ON: TELEVISION

I absolutely loved *The Goodies*; the opening sequence was enough to set me off laughing. My favourite episode was 'Kitten Kong', with Twinkle the giant cat on top of Post Office Tower and the Goodies dressed up as mice trying to catch it.

Author

The 'telly' was fast becoming a popular fixture in front rooms nationwide, especially as Britain had switched on to colour broadcasting in November 1969 with all three stations – BBC1, BBC2 and ITV – being transmitted in colour to most of the country. Television ownership was to rise throughout the decade to 20.2 million by April 1979, with an increase of 2.2 million households since 1970 owning their own set compared to those who rented one. Children were drawn to this technology, watching child-orientated programming, sports and family viewing, to the extent that some parents warned their offspring that they would get 'square eyes' if they watched too much.

Pre-school television viewers were generously catered for, with ITV and BBC channels airing an assortment of entertaining and educational programmes during weekday afternoons. Arguably, the most famous of ITV's pre-school viewing was *Rainbow*, first aired in 1972 with its puppet trio of quarrelsome Zippy, timid George and clumsy Bungle all kept

The Wombles could be found both overground and underground on Wimbledon Common. Left to right we have Madame Cholet, Tomsk, Bungo, Wellington, Great Uncle Bulgaria, Orinoco and Tobermory.

A young family with the 'goggle box' housed within its wooden veneered cabinet.

in order by the parental figure of Geoffrey. Alongside *Rainbow* was *Pipkins,* arriving on screen a year later with its puppets including the irascible Hartley Hare, Pig with his Brummie accent, and Topov the Cockney monkey. The BBC's early 1970s pre-school offerings comprised gentle, curious creations that captured the imagination of their young viewers: *Bagpuss, Mr Benn, Crystal Tipps and Alistair, Fingerbobs* and *Bod*; supplemented with those made in the late 1960s such as *Pogles' Wood, The Herbs* and the *Trumpton* series.

After-school viewing had to cater for a broad age range and, according to the television schedule for Wednesday 28 April 1976, the BBC had the head start, dedicating one hour forty minutes to child viewers in comparison to ITV's fifty-five minutes of scheduling. Starting off at 4:25pm on that particular day was ITV's *Runaround,* an energetic game show for kids filmed in front of a lively audience of youngsters and hosted by ebullient comedian Mike Reid; this was followed by a new half-hour drama series called *Westway,* about three families living in a commune in Bristol (very 'of the moment'). Over on BBC1, children's programmes commenced at 4:00pm with *Play School* and ended at 5:45pm with the *Magic Roundabout. Play School,* with its voice-over introduction 'A house with a door, One, two, three, four, Ready to play, What's the day?' and toys Humpty, Big and Little Teds, Hamble and Jemima, was aimed at both pre-school and reception age children. Based on song and storytelling, the programme had a raft of presenters who passed through its windows round, square and arched, with every child having their favourites among those who appeared on it throughout the decade, such as Brian Cant, Derek Griffiths and Floella Benjamin. The five-

BBC's *Blue Peter* presenters circa 1979. From left to right: Christopher Wenner, Lesley Judd, Goldie the golden retriever, Tina Heath and Simon Groom.

to ten-minute slot before the weekday evening news on BBC1 showcased some of the best in animated entertainment, with *The Clangers*, *Ivor the Engine*, *Captain Pugwash*, *The Wombles* and *Roobarb* all now perceived as prime examples of classic children's animation of the decade.

Programmes for older children notably included *Blue Peter,* which competed with ITV's trendy *Magpie*; the children's art programme *Take Hart* presented by Tony Hart ably assisted by Morph and *Ask Aspel* where children could write to the presenter Michael Aspel to request excerpts from television programmes. The decade's television was also dedicated to producing children's drama; *The Tomorrow People*, *Lizzie Dripping*, *The Adventures of Black*

Magpie's new presenter Jenny Handley being held aloft in 1974 by her fellow presenters Mick Robertson and Douglas Rae. Mick Robertson was television's answer to heart-throb singer David Essex.

The irrepressible Keith Chegwin and feline friend promote *Swap Shop*.

Beauty, *Just William* and *Children of the Stones* are just a few of the book adaptations and new screenplays that were televised. However, the drama that caught most children's imagination (whilst making some primary school children feel daunted at what lay ahead) was *Grange Hill*. First televised in 1978, the programme was set in the eponymous fictional comprehensive school where viewers were introduced to key pupil characters including 'Tucker' Jenkins, Benny Green, Trisha Yates and Penny Lewis – characters that viewers could relate to in everyday life. *Grange Hill* was ground-breaking television, portraying school life in a realistic light and broaching sensitive issues affecting secondary school age children nationwide. From friendship troubles, puberty, bullying, racism, relationships and stealing, *Grange Hill* didn't shy away from

'Seconds away, round two' – the kids' favourite: Big Daddy (aka Shirley Crabtree) slams 'baddie' Giant Haystacks (aka Martin Ruane) down in the ring to thunderous applause and cheers from grapple fans.

gritty storylines, although these were alleviated by humour, usually at the teachers' expense and the viewers' satisfaction.

The morning of Saturday 5 January 1974 on ITV was a pivotal moment when it came to children's weekend television programmes, for it introduced the first episode of *Tiswas*. Short for 'Today Is Saturday Watch And Smile', *Tiswas* didn't just rewrite the rule book on children's entertainment: it threw a bucket of water over it and flung a flan on top for good measure. Presenter Chris Tarrant's catchphrase of 'This is what they want' before throwing a bucket of water at an excited group of children is exactly what the viewers wanted. *Tiswas* made Saturday mornings memorable. It was anarchic, madcap, unpredictable humour, which could end in a child member of the audience in tears, a famous pop singer being pie'd in the face by the Phantom Flan Flinger or just the presenters and audience collapsing into utter mayhem. The BBC countered

Tom Baker as the new Dr Who for the popular BBC TV children's series. He is shown here with his long-standing enemies, the Daleks.

'It's good night from me and good night from him.' Saturday night's essential family viewing was the comedic genius of *The Two Ronnies*, which guaranteed belly laughs all round.

back in 1976 with the comparably restrained *Multi-Coloured Swap Shop* presented by disc jockey Noel Edmonds and co-presenters John Craven, Keith Chegwin, Maggie Philbin and a purple dinosaur soft-toy called Posh Paws. The premise of the programme comprised children phoning or writing into Edmonds requesting to swap toys and records for something else, with the swaps between children being matched up on the programme.

Saturday was family television time. The afternoon's favoured viewing was often sport, with wrestling one of the biggest draws. Known as 'grapple fans', the audience – both in person and at home – would cheer on their favourites from the pantheon of wrestling greats: the masked Kendo Nagasaki, Mick McManus in his black briefs, shaggy-haired Catweazel, stolid Giant Haystacks and (the grannies' and children's favourite) Big Daddy who entered into the ring alongside chants of 'Ea-sy, ea-sy'. If the wrestling wasn't action enough, the sight of an elderly audience member leaving her seat and thwacking the 'baddie' opponent with her handbag from the side of the ring would raise a giggle or two.

The evening's entertainment started at tea-time with *Dr Who*, played by Jon Pertwee between 1970 and 1974, with Tom Baker following as the fourth Time Lord incarnation who seamlessly took over the role for the rest of the decade with his distinctly bohemian air, mop of curls, trademark floppy fedora and long stripy scarf. Cue many children hiding behind the sofa or watching with their hands held warily over their eyes as the Doctor and his assistants battled against myriad devious foes. From the Daleks commanded by the hideous Davros, to the egg-headed Sontarans and the green-tentacled Krynoid, children were thrilled, engrossed and scared in equal measure by the alien hordes that the Doctor had to contend with in each series.

The 1970s produced a host of memorable family entertainment programmes. *The Generation Game* presented by the genial Bruce Forsythe whose opening 'Nice to see you, to see you ...' to which the live audience replied 'Nice!' had families shouting out the prizes appearing on the television as they passed on the conveyor belt before the contestant's eyes. The contestant had to remember as many prizes as possible, including the obligatory cuddly toy and fondue set. Also piling on the laughs were comedies like *Fawlty Towers, Are You Being Served?, Some Mothers Do 'Ave 'Em, The Goodies* and the comedians themselves: Dick Emery, Eric Sykes, Tommy Cooper and the enduring brilliance of double acts Morecombe and Wise and the two Ronnies, Corbett and Barker. Programmes such as these excelled at bringing the family together in one room, bonded by shared humour that easily rendered a family helpless with gales of hysterical laughter.

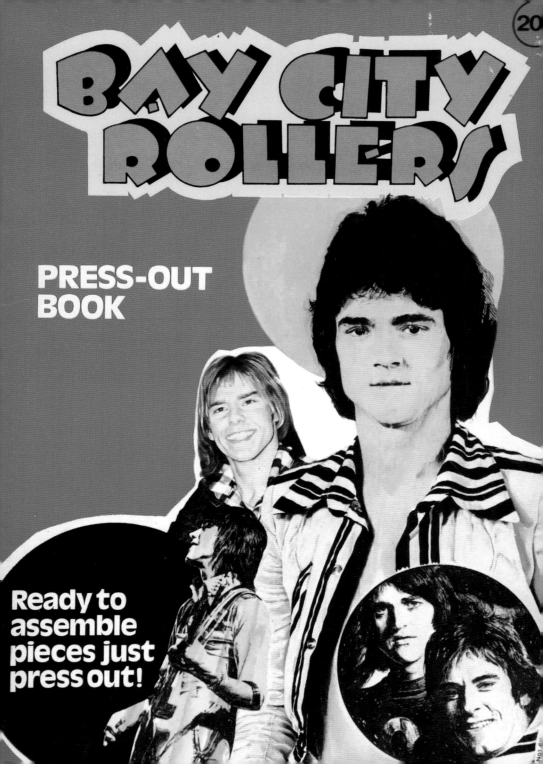

THE BEAT GOES ON: POPULAR MUSIC

In 1977 some young upstart decided to do a middle-class rebellion by graffitiing 'Sham 69' – the name of a punk band – onto the neighbours' fence. The horror! Everyone helped them scrub the graffiti off, but the irony was that until a couple of years ago you could still see it every time it rained – and it rains a lot in Scotland!

Gilly Ballard

The 1970s was one of the most vibrant and diverse decades for both British popular music and youth culture. It spanned numerous genres, which allowed youngsters to express their own individuality whilst allying themselves to a youth movement, giving them the freedom to dress and act how they wanted, being part of a wider 'family' and distinctive social group. The musical tastes of older siblings, encompassing heavy, progressive and glam rock, through to mainstream pop, reggae, punk, northern soul and disco, also played their part in influencing their younger brothers and sisters. It would be these formative influences that in turn would form the bedrock for future decades of popular music.

The initial introduction to pop music for young children in the 1970s was likely to have been via the radio, possibly listening to *Junior Choice* on BBC Radio 1, first appearing on the airwaves in the early 1950s. Children could request their own choice of music from popular songs, classical music and

The Bay City Rollers were a teenybopper pop sensation, generating a variety of merchandise from tartan scarves through to fan magazines.

Slick and athletic dance moves were all part of the 1970s northern soul scene.

'Keep a little Marc in your heart' – the tousle-haired electric warrior himself, T Rex's Marc Bolan playing some boogie with Steve Currie on bass and percussionist Micky Finn on *Top of the Pops*.

hymns to be featured on the programme. Yet by 1970 *Junior Choice* had moved with the times and adapted its playlist to suit a new generation's musical tastes. Presented by the avuncular Ed 'Stewpot' Stewart with his trademark greeting, 'Mornin'', his popularity would see him DJ-ing the programme throughout the decade. *Junior Choice* stalwarts typified by Charles Penrose's 'Laughing Policeman' (1926) and 'The Trail of the Lonesome Pine' (1937) by Laurel and Hardy were still on rotation, but were now jostled by cheekier comedic newcomers Terry Scott in schoolboy incarnation 'My Brother' (1962) and Benny Hill in full-on nudge-nudge-wink-wink mode, with 'Ernie (The Fastest Milkman in the West)' (1971). These songs were slotted in between contemporary tunes from pop groups such as Middle of the Road ('Chirpy Chirpy Cheep Cheep', 1971) and the Bay City Rollers ('Bye Bye Baby', 1975); interspersed with Stewart's giggle-worthy jingles: 'Ello Darlin' and the infamous 'Happy birthday to you, squashed tomatoes and stew…'

The decade also saw the rise of the teenybopper: essentially pre-teen and teenage girls fixated on pop stars including Marc Bolan and Davids Bowie and Essex. As one former teenybopper recalls:

My firm favourites were Kenny, the Bay City Rollers and David Essex. Marc Bolan had his own TV show and I remember watching him dressed in leopard skin lounging on a velvet settee – all very intriguing to an eight-year-old.

There were also American imports in the form of Leif Garrett, The Jackson 5 and undoubtedly the most popular of all, David Cassidy, whose poster-perfect flicked hair

and gleaming white smile adorned numerous bedroom walls. Public appearances and concerts by these pop stars turned into absolute pandemonium as girls screamed, fainted and pushed each other out of the way to get a glimpse of, or touch, their idol. Concerts turned into scream-fests as the music was drowned out by baying fans, which no doubt frustrated the performers. The risk of becoming crushed was an actual threat, as realised at a concert at London's White City Stadium in 1974, where a fourteen-year-old girl was caught up amongst a surging hysterical mass of David Cassidy fans. When retrieved from the crowd the girl was found to be alive but unconscious; sadly, she never regained consciousness and died days later.

The first half of the 1970s ushered in the rock 'supergroup' with Led Zeppelin, Black Sabbath, Queen and Deep Purple cutting a swathe through the music scene with a barrage of guitar riffs, drum solos and charismatic vocalists. Selling out venues not only in Britain but worldwide, these bands were inadvertently writing the aural and visual blueprint for the future of heavy rock. Yet by mid-decade, this rock behemoth was starting to lose its stride, being overtaken by punk, mainstream pop and disco. However, teenagers disillusioned with the recession's effects on both job choices and their personal lives, sought to imitate this former supergroup glory

Excited scarf-waving David Cassidy fans get ready to greet him at his White City Stadium concert in May 1975.

NWOBHM lads head-banging and playing air guitar – a scene that could be found in youth clubs and school discos throughout the UK in the late 1970s.

that, for the lucky few, could lead to a literal high life of fame and fortune. Hosts of new heavy rock bands were springing up; their influences comprised supergroup rock injected with vigour from the contemporary punk scene. This musical influx was referred to as the New Wave of British Heavy Metal (NWOBHM) and found a welcome home on bedroom turntables, stitched onto the backs of denim jackets and inked on the covers of school exercise books. With their livery of leather and denim jackets, band logo T-shirts, studded belts and long hair, pre-teen and teenage followers of heavy metal could be found shaking their heads in time to the music – head-banging – and playing air guitar, totally engrossed in the music and the atmosphere of the scene.

The presence of women in '70s rock and pop was more often than not confined to fronting an all-male band as evinced by ABBA's Agnetha Fältskog and Anni-Frid Lyngstad, bassist Suzi Quatro and Vinegar Joe's Elkie Brooks, or as part of a duo, Peters and Lee for example. Soloists like Lynsey de Paul and Joan Armatrading had to vie for chart space with an overwhelmingly male contingent. Even with outstanding vocal and musical ability, women had to fight for their place in this male-dominated world and whilst boys had their male rock stars to look up to and emulate, girls were more limited for radical female musician role models. It would take the onslaught of punk rock to give women a more equal stage on which to compete with their male counterparts. In doing so, innovative and diverse role models came to the fore in the form of Siouxsie Sioux, The Slits and Poly Styrene from X-Ray Spex. These women and others like them challenged the music industry norm of having to be pretty, feminine and compliant in order to sell records. Bursting out onto high streets throughout Britain in 1976 and spearheaded by the Sex Pistols, punk was set against a backdrop of inflation, the tail-end of a three-year recession and the hottest heatwave on record. Its do-it-yourself ethos of music and fashion, where individualism and anti-establishment views were celebrated, provided youngsters with an original and expressive musical genre and sub-culture to belong to.

Boisterous punks displaying a traditional salutation. On Saturday afternoons it was usual to see throngs of punks congregating in town centres the length and breadth of Britain.

The polar opposite to punk was disco. It took the hit film *Saturday Night Fever* (1978) to ignite the mainstream interest in discos and the high-energy rhythms that typified the genre. Disco music proliferated into school and youth club discos where youngsters danced to the film's soundtrack provided by the Bee Gees and songs like '*Rasputin*' (Boney M, 1978), '*YMCA*' (The Village People, 1978), '*Can You Feel the Force?*' (The Real Thing, 1979) and '*Le Freak*' (Chic, 1979).

When nineteen-year-old Kate Bush appeared in early 1978 with her chart-topping debut single '*Wuthering Heights*', people were either transfixed or repelled by her falsetto vocals, the latter writing her off as a one-hit wonder soon to be relegated to the 'Where Are They Now?' files. Yet the originality of Bush's music and visual performance earned her a fast-growing fanbase, especially amongst younger fans where her musical persona equally fascinated boys and girls. The sensuality of Bush's promotional photos appealed to her male admirers whilst her crimped hair and heavy make-up was avidly copied by female fans. With two albums released in 1978 and a sell-out nationwide tour in 1979 receiving widespread critical acclaim, Bush had in less than two years established herself as one of Britain's foremost female singer-songwriters.

YOU WEAR IT WELL: FASHION

I think it was 1976 when I was seven, that mum took me
to Woolworths and brought me a white nylon T-shirt with
a Bay City Rollers transfer on the front. I was so excited
– a fashionable T-shirt at last!

Author

While trendy mums may have dressed their offspring in
clothes from the children's department of 'Big' Biba in
London's Kensington High Street, the majority of Britain's
mums had to sew clothing from scratch or rely on hand-
me-downs from friends and family: 'We were more likely
to wear hand-me-downs than anything else. In fact, we
probably had no idea what a brand was.' If the housekeeping
could stretch to it, these clothes were supplemented with
occasional new items from high street shops, typically
British Home Stores, C&A and Littlewoods. Shopping
at home via a catalogue like Kays or Great Universal was
popular too, especially as they operated schemes whereby
clothes could be paid for by weekly instalments, very
welcome in homes where every penny in a weekly wage
packet had to be accounted for. With the exception of
private preparatory schools, most children of primary
school age didn't wear a uniform, just their usual 'civvies'.
This emphasised the divide between those whose parents
could afford to dress them in 'first-hand' clothes and the

Examples of
the exuberant
creations
crocheted by
well-meaning
relatives, but
more often
than not
unappreciated by
their recipients.

Child models wearing clothes from the *British Home Stores* children's range. 'Mini-me' clothes as seen in countless family wedding photos.

children who were poorly dressed in ill-fitting second-hand clothes that had seen better days.

Children's clothes in the early 1970s reflected aspects of contemporary fashions that their parents wore. The trend for miniskirts even extended to little girls' dresses and it was common to see them wearing ultra-short dresses accessorised with white lacy tights and T-bar sandals. Correspondingly, floor-length maxi skirts and dresses were also worn by both women and girls. Made from cotton or crimplene, these dresses had an evident sense of nostalgia about them with their puffed sleeves, high necklines and frills that evoked not only the fashions of the Victorian and Edwardian eras as translated by British fashion designer Laura Ashley, but also the printed dresses and pinafores from the popular American television series *Little House on the Prairie*. As with adults, flares in denim or corduroy were popular for boys and girls, teamed with a brightly patterned cotton T-shirt or a polyester shirt or blouse. Trouser suits were also worn by both sexes, comprising a pair of trousers with a matching tailored jacket complete with wide lapels; the author can remember wearing a brushed denim trouser suit with bell-bottom flares and patch pockets on the jacket – all home sewn as my parents couldn't afford an off-the-peg version.

The 1970s was arguably *the* decade for clothes manufacturing using man-made fibres. Clothes fashioned from fabrics like nylon and crimplene were convenient for busy mums as they dried quickly and needed no ironing – although the feeling of acrylic that hadn't been softened with fabric conditioner could easily put a child's teeth on edge. Similarly, many a young neck was also irritated by an itchy acrylic polo-neck

The author wearing a very short dress made by her mum. Note the typical sandals-and-socks combo popular at the time.

jumper that no amount of stretching could pull out of shape to aid the wearer's comfort. When getting undressed for bed in the dark, it could be exciting to watch the crackling sparks of static electricity spring forward from taking off a combination of acrylic jumper and nylon vest, but it was no fun getting a sharp unexpected static shock from touching metal or another man-made fibre-clad person. However, there was also a serious health and safety aspect with the use of these textiles for clothing. It was common for children's nightclothes and dressing gowns to be manufactured from fabrics like brushed cotton and nylon which, though cosy and soft-to-the-touch, were highly flammable. Central heating was a luxury that not many working families could afford as most homes were heated by bulky night storage heaters or an open fire, both commonly supplemented with electric bar radiators. In chilly houses it was the norm for children to stand in front of the fire to get dressed or go to bed with a bar radiator nearby, yet these posed a great risk of clothing – especially nightdresses – coming into contact with naked flames or the radiator's exposed element

This young pop fan is proudly wearing a T-shirt emblazoned with the face of Little Jimmy 'Long Haired Lover From Liverpool' Osmond.

and subsequently catching fire. This was especially relevant during the 1979 Winter of Discontent where candles were relied upon for light and paraffin heaters for warmth. The Nightdresses (Safety) Regulations had been previously issued in 1967 by Her Majesty's Stationery Office and by the early 1970s nightdresses and dressing gowns were made of low flammability fabrics or labelled if they were not made using flame-retardant material.

The economic effects of the recession, in conjunction with a boom in handicrafts, saw many children clothed in handmade garments. Local haberdashery shops kept a variety of pattern catalogues that their customers could rifle through for their intended sewing pattern choice and every town had a wool shop. Cardigans, jumpers and accessories were knitted by family members for younger children, being invaluable in supplementing clothes where money was tight. The '70s also saw a boom in crochet, with patterns abounding for children's ponchos, waistcoats, tank tops and dresses pieced together from colourful 'granny squares' crocheted from scratchy acrylic yarn. Far trendier homemade clothes were those from Clothkits, whose trademark comprised simple outfits like A-line skirts, pinafore dresses and trousers in bright colours with stylised folk-art motifs. A mail-order company, Clothkits made home sewing easier by selling a do-it-yourself kit, which did away with the traditional paper pattern. Instead the pattern was printed direct onto the reverse of the fabric, usually cotton or corduroy. And once the pieces were cut out, all that was needed was to sew them together.

The anorak was a unisex item of clothing that most children of the decade probably wore at some point. They came in an assortment of colours, but the one that sticks out the most was the navy-blue quilted version with its elasticated cuffs (bearing evidence that its wearer had a runny nose), metal zip that more often than not became snagged on a jumper, and plastic toggles on a long nylon cord, which inevitably ended up being chewed out of recognition. The navy blue

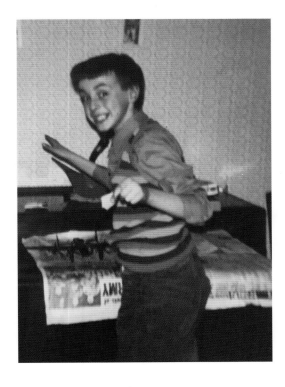

A cheerful young man wearing a colourful hand-knitted tank top in polyester.

or green nylon snorkel jacket or 'parka' with its orange lining was another parental favourite due to its practicality over style and that it could be bought cheap from the local market. The parka was also favoured by school bullies who could drag their unwilling victims around the playground by the deep, fake-fur-lined hood. Add to this list the trendy bomber jacket and the ubiquitous duffle coat (no thanks to Paddington Bear) with its toggles and you more or less have the line-up of a typical '70s school cloakroom.

Essential footwear teamed with the anorak were plimsolls, otherwise known as 'daps', supplemented with wellies for rainy days or playing about in streams. For school, the classic T-bar shoe or sandal in leather or patent leather was a popular choice for girls; T-bar sandals were also worn by boys typified by Clarks' brown leather Brutus sandals or the Rustler with

All the young dudes. A group of fashionable teens with their fringes, collar-length hair, flares and bomber jackets.

its perforated decoration. However, a common shoebox horror was the chunky brown leather lace-up Polyveldt shoe with its 'pie crust' or 'pasty' ridged toe seam, its practicality and robustness appealing more to the parental purse than its wearer. These sturdy and virtually invincible shoes could withstand rough and ready playground football and intentional scuffing by those who preferred Clarks' other stablemates: the Wayfinder with its soles imprinted with animal prints and a built-in compass secreted in the heel, or the Commandos, which came with a free button badge emblazoned with a 'C' in a military-style font. The 'beetlecrusher' shoe with its crepe flat sole, as influenced by rock 'n' roll bands of the day like Mud and Showaddywaddy, was another favourite, endowing its wearers with an edge of street credibility over their pie-crust-shod peers.

EPILOGUE

This concludes a time-travelling hour or so spent reminiscing about misspent youth or, for younger readers, perhaps an introduction into the formative years of their parents and grandparents. Hopefully it has brought back some fun memories of daily family life, and even perhaps those of hardship, where life wasn't as rosy as depicted in family sit-coms.

Lastly, I apologise if I haven't managed to include the reader's favourite memories of the 1970s; there was a risk that this book might purely turn into itemised lists instead of a broad retrospective of the decade. However, I have endeavoured to include both objects and brands that are commonly associated with the decade and also less obvious examples – ones that will, I hope, trigger those forgotten memories of a decade that to many seems like yesterday once more.

FURTHER READING

Kibble-White, Graham (Ed.). *TV Cream: The Ultimate Guide to 70s and 80s Pop Culture*. Virgin Books, 2005.

Moss, Elaine. *The Seventies in Children's Books*. First published in *The Signal Approach to Children's Books*. Kestrel, 1980.

Sandbrook, Dominic. *A State of Emergency. The Way We Were: Britain 1970–1974*. Penguin Books, 2011.

Sandbrook, Dominic. *Seasons in the Sun*. Allen Lane, 2012.

The Best of Jackie Annual. Prion, 2006.

Viner, Brian. *Nice to See It, To See It, Nice*. Pocket Books, 2010.

IMAGE ACKNOWLEDGEMENTS

Images are gratefully acknowledged as follows: Anne Banerji, Page 59; Caroline Greville-Morris/Redferns/Getty Images, page 53; CM Dixon/Heritage Images/Getty Images, page 30; Eamonn McCabe/Redferns/Getty Images, page 44 (bottom); Evening Standard/Getty Images, pages 11, 17, 18, 19, 23, 28, 36, 51, 56; Fin Costello/Redferns/Getty Images, page 44 (top); Fox Photos/Getty Images, page 12; GAB Archive/Redferns/Getty Images, page 46 and 48; Graham Wood/Evening Standard/Getty Images, page 14; Jan Gardner, pages 1, 25, 31 (both), 58; John Bulmer/Getty Images, page 26; Keystone/Getty Images, page 15; Keystone/Hulton Archive/Getty Images, page 43 (bottom); Liza Hollinghurst, page 57; Martin O'Neill/Redferns/Getty Images, page 10; McCarthy/Daily Express/Getty Images, page 24; Michael Putland/Getty Images, page 45; Mick Gold/Redferns/Getty Images, page 50 (top); Monti Spry/Central Press/Hulton Archive/Getty Images, page 37; Oliver Morris/Getty Images, page 32 (top); Photofusion/UIG via Getty Images, page 16; Popperfoto/Getty Images, page 9; PYMCA/UIG via Getty Images, page 32 (bottom); Reg Lancaster/Express/Getty Images, page 60; Rolls Press/Popperfoto/Getty Images, page 8; Ron Howard/Redferns/Getty Images, page 50 (bottom); Science & Society Picture Library/Getty Images, page 20, 29; Steve Lewis/Getty Images, pages 6, 22; Susan Wood/Getty Images, page 54; Tony Evans/Getty Images, page 40; Twentieth Century Fox Pictures/Sunset Boulevard/Corbis via Getty Images, page 33; United News/Popperfoto/Getty Images, page 43 (top); Universal/Getty Images, page 35; Victor Drees/Evening Standard/Getty Images, page 42; Virginia Turbett/Redferns/Getty Images, page 52.

PLACES TO VISIT

Black Country Living Museum, Tipton Road, Dudley, West Midlands DY1 4SQ. Telephone: 0121 557 9643. Website: www.bclm.co.uk

Brighton Toy and Model Museum, 52–55 Trafalgar Street, Brighton, Sussex BN1 4EB. Telephone: 01273 749494. Website: www.brightontoymuseum.co.uk

The Geffrye Museum of the Home, 136 Kingsland Road, London E2 8EA. Telephone: 020 7739 9893. Website: www.geffrye-museum.org.uk

Highland Museum of Childhood, The Old Station, Strathpeffer, IV14 9DH. Telephone: 01997 421031. Website: www.s620947988.websitehome.co.uk

Museum of Brands, Packaging & Advertising, 111–117 Lancaster Road, Notting Hill, London W11 1QT. Telephone: 0207 243 9611. Website: www.museumofbrands.com

Museum of Childhood, 42 High Street, Royal Mile, Edinburgh EH1 1TB. Telephone: 0131 529 4142. Website: www.edinburghmuseums.org.uk/venue/museum-childhood

Sudbury Hall and the National Trust Museum of Childhood, Sudbury Hall, Main Road, Sudbury, Ashbourne, Derbyshire DE6 5HT. Telephone: 01283 585337. Website: www.nationaltrust.org.uk/sudbury-hall-and-the-national-trust-museum-of-childhood

V&A Museum of Childhood, Cambridge Heath Road, London E2 9PA. Telephone: 020 8983 5200. Website: www.vam.ac.uk/moc

West Wales Museum of Childhood, Pen-ffynnon, Llangeler, Carmarthenshire SA44 5EY. Telephone: 01559 370428. Website: www.toymuseumwales.co.uk

INDEX

Page numbers in Italics refer to illustrations

ABBA 52
Action Man 28, **29**, 30
Adventures of Black Beauty, The 43–4
Airfix 30
Angel Delight 24
Arctic Roll 24
Are You Being Served? 47
Ashley, Laura 56
Bagpuss 42
Baker, Tom **45**, 47
Barbie 28, 30
Bay City Rollers **48**, 50, 55
Beano, The 37
Bee Gees 53
Benjamin, Floella 42
Benn, Mr 42
Berni Steakhouse 24
Bicycles 5, 25, **25**, 31, **31**
Bionic Woman 30
Black Sabbath 51
Bolan, Marc 50, **50**
Boney M 53
Bowie, David 50
Blue Peter 43, **43**
Bod 42
Bomber jacket 59, **60**
British Home Stores 55, **56**
Brooks, Elkie 52
Bunty 38
Bush, Kate 53
Cadbury's 24
Candlewick 9
Captain Pugwash 43
Carrie's War 35
Cassidy, David 50–1, **51**
Catweazle 46
Chad Valley 9
Chegwin, Keith **44**, 46
Children of the Stones 44
Clackers 30
Clangers, The 43
Clothkits 58–9
Crabtree, Shirley ('Big Daddy') **44**, 46–7
Crochet **55**, 58
Cooper, Tommy 47
Crystal Tipps and Alistair 42
Dahl, Roald 5, 35
    Charlie and the Glass Elevator 35
Dandy, The 37
Deep Purple 51
Dental health 22
Diddakoi, The 35
Disco 49, 53
Downfall 31, **31**
Dr Who **45**, 47
Duffle coat 59
Elizabeth II, Queen 7–9, 9
Emery, Dick 47
Essex, David 43, 50
Fanta 21
Father Abraham 5

Fawlty Towers 47
Fingerbobs 42
Forsythe, Bruce 47
Generation Game, The 47
Girl's World 29, 30
Goal! 38
Gonks 30
Goodies, The 41, 47
Goldie the Golden Retriever **43**
Great Universal 55
Grange Hill 44–5
Green Shield Stamps 27
Griffiths, Derek 42
Groom, Simon **43**
Hamleys 28, **28**
Hargreaves, Roger 37, **37**
    Mr Tickle 37
Hart, Tony 43
Heath, Tina **43**
Heatwave 7–8, **8**, 31
Herbs, The 42
Hill, Benny 50
Hobbie, Holly 9
Hot Rod Racers 30
Hyde Park 19, **19**
Ivor the Engine 43
Jackie 39
James, Sid 30, 38
Judd, Lesley **43**
Junior Choice 49–50
Just William 44
Keegan, Kevin 32
Ladybird Books 34, 35–6
Laurel and Hardy **50**
Led Zeppelin 51
Lee, Bruce 25, 30
Lego 13, **29**, 30
Legs & Co. 5
Little House on the Prairie 56
Lizzie Dripping 43
Look-In 37
Mandy 38
Magic Roundabout 42
Magpie 43, **43**
Marvel Comics 38
Masquerade 39
Middle of the Road 50
Milky Bar Kid 22
Misty 38
Morecombe and Wise 47
Morph 43
Mud 60
Multi-Coloured Swap Shop **44**, 46
National Union of School Students 17
New Wave of British Heavy Metal 52, **52**
Northern Soul 49, **50**
Notting Hill Adventure Playground 30, **30**
Osmond, Little Jimmy **58**
Osmonds, The 39
Pertwee, Jon 47
Peters and Lee 52
Pink Floyd 5
Pipkins 42

Pippa 28
Play School 42
Pleasance, Donald 32
Pogles' Wood 42
Posh Paws 46
Punk 49, 52–3, **53**
Quatro, Suzi 52
Queen 51
Quintin Kynaston School 19
Rae, Douglas **43**
Railway Children, The 35, **35**
Real Thing, The 53
Rainbow 41
Robertson, Mick **43**
Roobarb 43
Roy of the Rovers 38
Ruane, Martin ('Giant Haystacks') **44**, 46
Runaround 42
Saturday Night Fever 53
Scalextrix **29**, 30
School
    Assemblies 17; Corporal Punishment
    17, 19; Demonstrations 19, **19**;
    Free Milk 18, **18**; Lunches 14,
    15–16; Playgrounds **12**, 14–15;
    Teachers 16–17
Sex Pistols 53
Sham 69: 49
Shoes 56, 57, 59–60
Showaddywaddy 60
Silver Jubilee 7–9, **9**
Simon (game) 28
Sindy 28, **29**
Six Million Dollar Man 30, 38
Slade 27
Slits, The 52
Smoking 23, **23**
SodaStream **20**, 25
Some Mothers Do 'Ave 'Em 47
Star Wars 5, 28, 33, **33**
Stewart, Ed 'Stewpot' 50
Styrene, Poly 52
Sweets 5, 16, 21, 22–3
Take Hart 43
Tarrant, Chris 45
Thatcher, Margaret 18
Thin Lizzy 39
Tiswas 45
Tomorrow People, The 43
Top of the Pops 5, **50**
Trumpton 42
Twinkle 38
Two Ronnies, The 5, **46**, 47
Valiant 38
Village People, The 53
Watership Down 35
Wenner, Christopher **43**
Winter of Discontent 58
Wombles, The 4, **40**, 41, 43
Woolworths 9, 27, 55
X-Ray Spex 52